Classifyin [plants]
and Animals

by Camille La Vouché

PEARSON
Scott
Foresman

DK

What are the building blocks of life?

What Cells Are

A **cell** is the smallest unit of a living thing. A cell can carry out life functions. All living things are made of cells. Some are made of one cell. Plants and animals have many cells. Cells are the building blocks of life.

Cells have jobs. Cells can help a living thing use energy, grow, and reproduce. Some cells keep a living thing healthy. Cells can develop only from other cells.

You can use microscopes to see cells. A microscope makes objects look bigger than they are. Scientists look at cells through a microscope. Then they learn many things about cells.

A microscope helps scientists see the details of a cell.

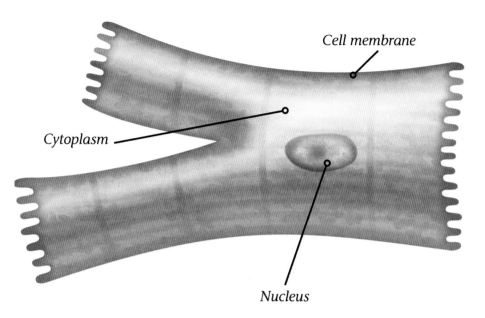

Cell membrane

Cytoplasm

Nucleus

The size and shape of a cell are related to the cell's job.

The Parts of a Cell

Animals such as eagles and elephants do not look alike. They are made of cells. These cells have parts that are alike. Each part of a cell has a job.

Plant cells and animal cells have a nucleus, cytoplasm, and a cell membrane. The **nucleus** tells the cell what to do. **Cytoplasm** is a gel-like material. It has what the cell needs to do its job. The cell membrane is the border of the cell. It separates the cell from what is outside of it.

Cells Working Together

Cells are organized into groups. Different groups of cells do different jobs.

Cells that do the same job form tissues. A group of tissues that work together forms an organ. The heart is an organ. Organs that work together to do a job are called organ systems. The heart is one part of an organ system.

An organism is a complete living thing. It is the highest level of cell organization.

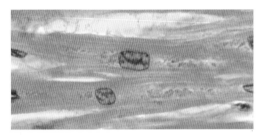

A group of one kind of cell is a tissue. Each kind of tissue does a certain job.

A group of tissues that work together is an organ. The heart is one organ in an animal.

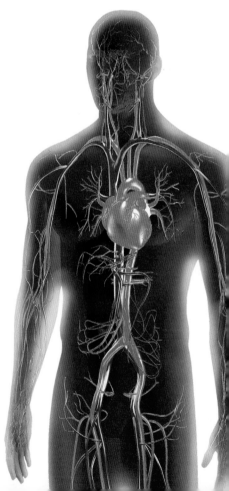

Many organs work together in an organ system. The heart, blood, and blood vessels are some parts of one system.

Plant cells have parts that animal cells do not have. Plant cells have chloroplasts. A **chloroplast** traps energy from the Sun. This energy helps the plant make its own food.

Each plant cell has a cell wall. The cell wall is a layer outside the cell membrane. It supports the plant cell. It also protects the plant cell.

A Plant Cell

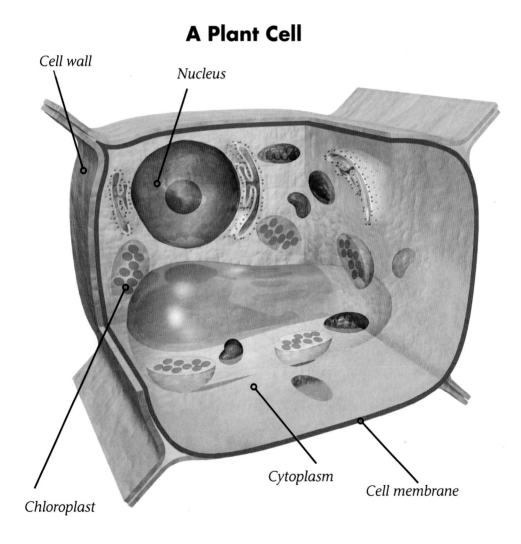

Cell wall

Nucleus

Chloroplast

Cytoplasm

Cell membrane

How are living things grouped?

Classification Systems

Scientists sort living things into groups. Organisms in the same group have things in common.

Kingdoms

A kingdom is the largest classification group. Many scientists classify organisms into six kingdoms.

Dandelions

Answer these questions to see if a dandelion and a mushroom are in the same kingdom. How many cells does the organism have? Where does it live? How does it get food?

They both have more than one cell. They both live on land and grow in soil. A dandelion makes its own food. A mushroom takes in food from other things.

Dandelions and mushrooms are alike in some ways. But they do not get their food in the same way. They are not in the same kingdom.

Mushrooms

Kingdoms of Living Things

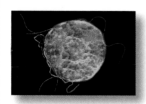

Ancient Bacteria
Ancient bacteria are made of one cell. They have no separate nucleus. They live in water or on land. They make their own food.

True Bacteria
True bacteria have one cell. They have no separate nucleus. They live in water or on land. Some get food. Others make their own food.

Protists
Most protists have one cell. They have a nucleus and other cell parts. Some get food. Others make their own. Algae and paramecia are protists.

Fungi
Fungi have many cells. Each cell has a nucleus and other parts. Fungi absorb food from other living or nonliving things. They live on land. Mushrooms are fungi.

Plants
Plants have many cells. Each cell has a nucleus and other parts. The cells form tissues and organs. Plants live on land or in water. They use sunlight to make food. Dandelions are plants.

Animals
Animals have many cells. The cells make up tissues, organs, and organ systems. Animals live in water or on land. They eat plants and other animals.

Getting More Specific

Kingdoms are made up of smaller groups. Each group is then divided into smaller and smaller groups. Scientists use features of an organism to put it into groups.

Genus and species are the two smallest groups. They make up an organism's scientific name. A **genus** is a group of closely related plants or animals. A **species** is a group of similar organisms that can mate and produce offspring that can also produce offspring. The species name usually comes from a feature, such as the color of the organism or where it lives.

Members of the Cat Family

Most scientific names are Latin words. An animal's scientific name is the same all over the world. The house cat and the black-footed cat are both in the *Felis* genus. But they are different species. The house cat's species is *domesticus*, or "of the house." The black-footed cat's species is *nigripes*, or "black feet."

The scientific name of this house cat is *Felis domesticus*.

The scientific name of this black-footed cat is *Felis nigripes*.

The Animal Kingdom

Kingdom

Division

Class

Order

Family

Genus

Species

9

How are plants classified?

How Plants Transport Water And Nutrients

Bamboo is very tall. How do the cells at the top of this tall plant get water and nutrients from the soil? The plant has tubelike structures. The tubes bring water and nutrients to every part of the plant. Plants that have these tubes are called vascular plants. Grass, dandelions, and trees are vascular plants.

Vascular tissue also supports the plant's stems and leaves. The plant is able to grow larger.

Tubelike structures

The tissues of this bamboo slice can only be seen with a microscope.

More Down-to-Earth Plants

Plants that do not have tubelike structures are nonvascular plants. They cannot grow very tall. They do not have real roots, stems, or leaves. Water and nutrients move from one cell to the next cell.

Mosses

Mosses are the largest group of nonvascular plants. They make their own food. Some can live in low temperatures.

Hornworts

Hornworts do not have true stems or leaves. They tend to live in warm places.

Liverworts

Liverworts grow on moist rocks or soil by streams. Some have a spicy smell. Some look like flat leaves. Some have the shape of a liver.

How Plants Make New Plants

Scientists also classify plants by how they reproduce, or make new plants. Some plants reproduce using seeds. Other plants reproduce using spores.

Flowers and Seeds

Plants with flowers or cones make seeds. A seed has a young plant and food inside of it. Most seeds come from flowering plants. Seeds can have different shapes and sizes. A cactus, a fruit tree, and a poppy are flowering plants.

The pod of a soybean holds two or three seeds or beans.

Cones and Seeds

Conifers are plants that make seeds without flowers. Conifers grow cones. Some cones make pollen. Some cones make seeds. Evergreen plants are conifers. They do not lose their leaves, or needles, during the year.

A pine cone holds the seeds and pollen of a conifer.

Spores

Ferns and mosses are plants that do not make seeds. They make tiny cells. The tiny cells become new plants. These cells are called spores. A spore might become a new plant if it falls into a shady, moist place. It will get nutrients there.

Spore cases look like brown dots or streaks under a fern's leaves. The spore cases hold hundreds of spores.

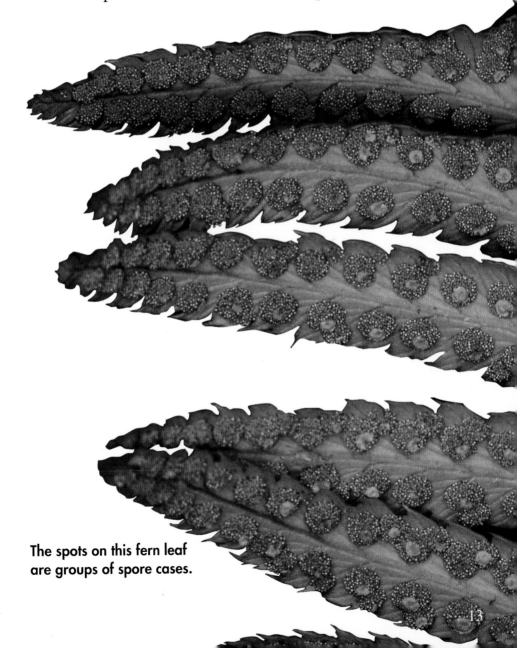

The spots on this fern leaf are groups of spore cases.

How are animals classified?

Animals with Backbones

The animal kingdom is made up of two groups. Animals that have backbones are in one group. They are called **vertebrates.** There are five kinds of vertebrates.

Vertebrates

Fish	Fish usually have scales. They live only in water. Fish get oxygen mostly with gills. Fish are cold-blooded. Most lay eggs.
Amphibians 	Amphibians are covered with moist skin. They live part of their life on land and part in the water. To breathe, they use lungs or gills or both. They are cold-blooded. Amphibians hatch from eggs.
Reptiles	Reptiles have scales. Most reptiles live on land. Some can live in water. They use lungs to breathe. Reptiles are cold-blooded. They usually lay eggs.
Birds	Birds have feathers. They usually live on land. Many birds spend much time in water. Birds use lungs to breathe. They are warm-blooded. All birds lay eggs.
Mammals 	Mammals have hair or fur. Most live on land. A few live in water. They breathe with lungs. Mammals are warm-blooded; they make their own heat. Most mammals have live births.

Reptiles

Reptiles are one group of vertebrates. They live in water and on land. Alligators, crocodiles, snakes, lizards, and turtles are reptiles. Reptiles have lungs for breathing. Their dry skin has scales or plates all over.

Alligators and crocodiles look alike. But they are different. The long teeth in an alligator's bottom jaw cannot be seen when its mouth is shut. A crocodile's teeth can be seen when its mouth is shut.

The python has a very long backbone.

15

Life Cycle of a Reptile

The Burmese python is a long, thick snake. It can be six meters (about twenty feet) long. It is not poisonous. It uses heat sensors on its upper lip to find food. It has a strong sense of smell. A python squeezes its prey and swallows it whole. The Burmese python can swallow animals whose bodies are larger than its own head.

A female python can lay as many as 100 eggs.

The mother python wraps herself around her eggs to keep them warm.

The young python hatches in about six to eight weeks.

The python grows and reproduces. It can live as long as 25 years.

Soon the mother leaves, and the young python must care for itself.

Invertebrates

Animals with no backbones are called **invertebrates.** Jellyfish, worms, spiders, snails, and clams are invertebrates. They have soft bodies.

Arthropods and More

Arthropods are animals with jointed legs. They are the largest group of invertebrates. Their legs and bodies are in sections. Insects, spiders, and crabs are arthropods. They have a hard, lightweight outer skin called an exoskeleton.

Spiders

Spiders are arthropods. They have eight legs. They have two main body parts. They can spin silk. Most spiders use this silk to make webs. Webs trap their prey.

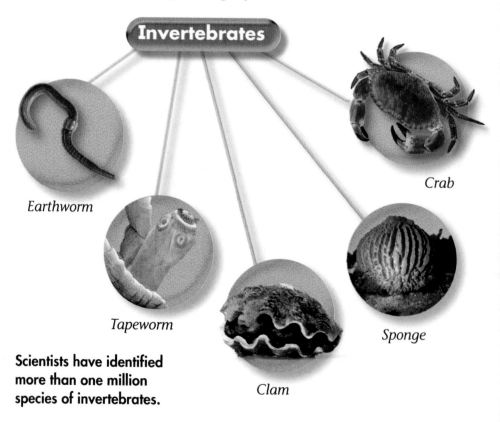

Invertebrates

Earthworm

Tapeworm

Crab

Clam

Sponge

Scientists have identified more than one million species of invertebrates.

A snail is a mollusk. It has a muscular structure called a foot. The foot oozes a slimy liquid. This helps the snail move. Some mollusks, such as oysters, do not move far. Some are good swimmers.

The largest invertebrate is the giant squid. It can be 15 meters, or 50 feet, long.

The Life Cycle of the Brown Snail

Mother snails dig nests to lay eggs. They can lay 85 eggs in a nest. The eggs hatch in two to four weeks. A newly-hatched snail has to get its own food. First, it will eat its own eggshell. It will then eat other eggs. Snails live for about ten years.

1. The brown garden snail lays its eggs.

2. The eggs hatch in two to four weeks.

3. Newly hatched snails must find food to grow.

4. Adult snails reproduce and the life cycle begins again.

How do animals adapt?

How Animals Get What They Need

Young animals inherit traits, or physical features, from their parents. A physical feature or behavior that helps an animal survive and reproduce is an adaptation. All animals need food, water, oxygen, and shelter. Animals that are adapted well have a better chance to survive and reproduce.

Birds' Adaptations

Birds have feathers that help them fly. The shapes of birds' beaks helps them get food. Ducks have webbed feet to help them swim.

Other Adaptations

Polar bears have thick coats of fur to keep them warm. They have sharp teeth and claws to catch and hold food.

Adaptations that Protect Animals

An animal's color can help it blend into its surroundings. This helps it hide from predators. A bright color can mean an animal is poisonous. Some animals have quills or hard shells for protection.

Blending In

Colors, shapes, and patterns can hide an animal. The rock ptarmigan has dark feathers in the summer. In the winter it has white feathers. It blends with the snow.

Rock ptarmigan in winter   *Rock ptarmigan in summer*

Protected by Poison

Some frogs and toads use poison for protection. The poison-dart frog's bright colors tell predators that it is dangerous. It can produce enough poison to kill a human!

Escaping Predators

Animals move in many ways to protect themselves. Some birds can fly away from predators. Fish have fins that help them swim away. Some animals can run for a long time.

Animal Instincts

Instincts are behaviors that animals inherit from parents. Instincts help animals meet their needs. Ducklings have the instinct to follow their mother. This is how they get food and protection.

Canada geese migrating

Migration

Food can be hard to find in places where the winter is cold. Migration is traveling to find food or a place to reproduce.

Migration can be difficult. Some amphibians may have to cross busy roads when they migrate. Some animals must travel long distances to escape the cold winter.

Hibernation and Inactivity

Some animals become inactive during very cold weather. This inactivity is called hibernation. It is an instinct. Some hibernating animals save energy by moving very little. Others do not move at all.

Bear hibernating

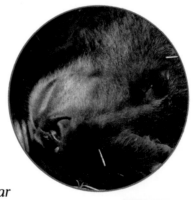

How Animals Learn

Some behavior must be learned. Young animals learn by watching their parents or other adults.

Parents Teach Offspring

Young animals can learn to hunt by watching their parents. A young lion practices pouncing on prey by pouncing on its mother's tail.

Offspring Teach Parents

Some adult animals learn from their young. A young monkey taught adult monkeys how to wash sand off their food.

Learned and Inherited

Some behaviors are inherited and learned. The white-crowned sparrow is born knowing how to sing. But it must learn the song its species sings.

Glossary

cell　　the smallest unit of a living thing that can carry out all life functions

chloroplast　　the part of a plant cell that traps energy from the Sun

cytoplasm　　the gel-like substance in a cell that has what the cell needs to do its job

genus　　a group of closely related living things

invertebrates　　animals without backbones

nucleus　　the control center of a cell

species　　a group of similar organisms that can mate and produce offspring that can also produce offspring

vertebrates　　animals with backbones